A

PRESERVATIVE

AGAINST

UNITARIANISM.

A

PRESERVATIVE

AGAINST

UNITARIANISM:

IN A LETTER TO

LANT CARPENTER, LL. D.

OCCASIONED BY HIS DISCOURSE,

DELIVERED AT BRISTOL,

BEFORE THE

SOCIETY OF UNITARIAN CHRISTIANS,

ESTABLISHED IN

THE WEST OF ENGLAND,

ENTITLED,

" ERRORS RESPECTING UNITARIANISM CONSIDERED; AND
" MOTIVES AND MEANS FOR THE DISSEMINATION OF
" IT STATED."

―――――

BY DANIEL VEYSIE, B. D.

Rector of Plymtree, Devon.

―――――

EXETER:

Printed by Trewman and Son;

SOLD BY RIVINGTONS, LONDON; PARKER, OXFORD; TREWMAN
AND DYER, EXETER; AND ALL OTHER BOOKSELLERS.

―――

1809.

A
Preservative against Unitarianism,

IN A LETTER TO

LANT CARPENTER, LL. D.

SIR,

THE Orthodox, as they are commonly called, are apt to charge the Unitarians with rejecting from Christianity almost all its peculiar doctrines, and with reducing it nearly to a level with natural religion. How far the Unitarians themselves either admit or deny this charge, is a point respecting which your Discourse seemed to promise ample information. But I confess that the perusal of it has not given me much satisfaction. It does not contain what I expected it to contain; or at least not so fully as I expected. From its title I was led to suppose that your object was, to give a clear and comprehensive exposition of the Unitarian doctrine, in order to vindicate it from the misrepresentations, and aspersions, under which it had laboured from the ignorance or malevolence of its adversaries; to prove that it is the true doctrine revealed in the Scriptures, and alone worthy of all acceptation; to point out the obstacles which at present impede its general reception; and lastly, to shew, that, if generally received, the necessary result would be, much glory to God, and much good to Man. You have, indeed, touched upon most of these points; but have treated none of them so clearly and fully as I had been led to expect. Nevertheless, as your Discourse has received the approbation of the Society before whom it was preached, and is now published at their desire, and under their sanction, its circulation will probably be as extensive as the influence of the Society can make it: and, therefore, a few remarks upon those parts more especially, which immediately relate to the Unitarian doctrine, may not be unseasonable.

It is difficult to say with precision what is Unitarianism. Even an Unitarian cannot speak of it without hesitation: for I perceive that you yourself, sir, labour under some difficulty in this respect. You express yourself upon many occasions with diffidence and caution; delivering not what you can boldly affirm to be the acknowledged doctrine of the sect to which you belong; but, what you *imagine* to be the general sentiment; (*Disc. p.* 9.) and what you *apprehend* to be the opinion of *at least a large proportion of your body.* *(Disc. p. 27.)* You have no settled creed, no determined points of doctrine, no articles of religion, to which you all assent, and to which your adversaries may appeal as the standard of your faith: but all is vague and uncertain. The opinions of some are indeed much more free than those of others: but, it is observable, that of the many prevailing errors respecting Unitarianism, which you notice in your Discourse, and labour to remove, there is hardly one, to which, by your own confession, the writings of Unitarians have not given occasion. But, if the Unitarians themselves give erroneous representations of Unitarianism, whence am I to learn what the true Unitarian doctrine is? and how, in general, am I to avoid the danger of asserting that to be Unitarianism, which I may, perhaps, be told is only the error of the individual, in whose writings I found it; but is not imputable to the body at large? This danger I can, indeed, upon the present occasion, contrive to avoid, by confining myself wholly to your Discourse: and I trust, that what I shall be able to collect from thence, you will not deny to be at least your Unitarianism, and that of the society to which you belong.

You profess to believe in the authority of the Scriptures: and though you reject the commonly received opinion respecting Inspiration (omitting, however, to state what this commonly received opinion is,) yet you admit that the books of the New Testament contain a faithful record of inspired doctrine: i. e. as you immediately explain your meaning, that the books of the New Testament contain a faithful record of the revelation of the will of God, communicated to mankind by Jesus Christ, either directly, or through the Apostles. *(Disc. p. 9.)* I will not dispute with you concerning the nature of Inspiration: I will be satisfied with your acknowledgement, that the record is *faithful*. Consequently no doctrine of human invention, however agreeable to reason, is to be received as Christian doctrine, unless it can be directly proved, or clearly inferred from the Scriptures: And, on the contrary, no doctrine, which can be so proved or inferred, is to be denied to be Christian doctrine, however apparently inconsistent with reason. Let but sufficient evidence be given that the thing proposed to our belief was taught by Christ or his Apostles, and it immediately becomes our duty, as you rightly declare, humbly to " exert ourselves to cast down " reasonings, and every high thing that exalts it- " self against the knowledge of God, and to bring " into captivity every thought to the obedience of " Christ." *(Disc. p. 11.)*

You admit that your brethren, in the zeal for what they deemed the important cause of Christian truth, " may occasionally have been led to adopt " modes of interpretation and criticism, which are " not to be justified by more rigid and correct " principles." *(Disc. p. 12.)* But you profess not to be of this number: if I rightly understand your meaning, you merely claim to yourself the privilege of departing from the commonly received translation, or from the commonly received Greek text, when the former appears not to have expressed the sense of the original with sufficient accuracy; or when the latter contains a reading, which, according to the rigid rules of sound criticism, ought not to have been admitted. If this be the whole for which you contend, you will, upon this point, meet with no opposition from me; nor, I am persuaded, from any of the members of the established Church; who all claim the same privilege, and scruple not to exercise it as often as occasion requires. Of this you cannot be ignorant. You know that the University of Oxford is now printing, at the Clarendon Press, the text of that indefatigable editor, whom you most admire: and the works of all our eminent divines plainly shew, that they are no more shackled by the opinion of the royal translators, than the Unitarians themselves. Why then such boasting, as though this ground were exclusively occupied by your own party? " As to this point " (say you) we think that we stand upon very high " ground." *(Disc. p. 15.)* Surely, sir, upon this point you are only upon a level with your neighbours: or if in any respect you stand upon higher ground, it is, not in the liberty which you enjoy, but in the use which you make of it. We are convinced (what you do not deny) that the commonly received text is generally, and especially in important points, correct; *(Disc. p. 14.)* and that the commonly received translation, which is founded upon it, is for the most part sufficiently faithful: we think, therefore, that it may be safely trusted in all matters, both of faith and of practice. But we do not forget, that, though the common Greek text is generally correct, it is still not perfect; and that, though the authorized translation is for the most part faithful, it is still not infallible. We therefore do not absolutely bind ourselves to either. But then we do not give way to a spirit of innovation: we proceed to the work of correction with humility and moderation; and never propose an alteration but in order to elucidate the true sense of a passage, and where the established rules of sound criticism will bear us out. The Unitarian, may, perhaps, come to the work with a bolder spirit, and a more daring hand. Eager to maintain his own opinions, he may suffer his prejudices, or, if you please, his zeal, to bias his judgment, and may be led to correct and interpret in a manner not altogether consistent with the principles of sound criticism. You deeply regret that any of your brethren should have given occasion to so serious a charge. But I am not sure that your own book does not afford some ground for imputing this charge even to yourself. I wish you seriously to consider whether your own interpretation of Scripture is always such as your unfettered and unbiassed judgement would approve: or whether your zeal in the cause of Unitarianism does not sometimes lead you to depart from the plain and obvious sense of a passage, in order to torture it into a meaning not altogether adverse to the opinions of your sect. I refer principally to your exposition of St. John, ch. i. 1, 3, 10, 14; also, ch. v. 23, and ch. viii. 58.

You give us a summary of the Unitarian belief in the four following propositions: viz.

1st. That Jesus of Nazareth was proved to be from God, by the miracles, and wonders, and signs, which God did by him:

2dly, That he was sent by God to bless men, by turning them away from their iniquities:

3dly, That after he had voluntarily submitted to a painful and ignominious death, as an attestation of the truth; God raised him from the dead, as an assurance of a future state of retribution: And

4thly. That through him forgiveness of sins is proclaimed to us. *(Disc. p. 6.)*

The two first of these propositions, and the last, are delivered nearly in the words of the texts of Scripture to which you refer in proof of them. Acts ii. 22—iii. 26—xiii. 38. They therefore call for no remark.

In the third proposition two things are asserted : 1st, That Jesus of Nazareth voluntarily submitted to a painful and ignominious death, as an attestation of the truth : 2dly, That God raised him from the dead, as an assurance of a future state of retribution.

In proof of the first of these assertions, you refer to John x. 18. "No man taketh it from me ; "but I lay it down of myself: I have power to "lay it down, and I have power to take it again." But this passage only proves that the death of Christ was voluntary : but by no means that his death was intended primarily and principally as an attestation of the truth.

In proof of the second assertion, you refer to Acts xvii. 31. "Because he hath appointed a day, "in the which he will judge the world in righte- "ousness by that man whom he hath ordained ;

" whereof he hath given assurance unto all men,
" in that he hath raised him from the dead." But
the thing directly asserted in this place, is, that
the person, by whom God will hereafter judge the
world, is the same whom he hath raised from the
dead; and that his resurrection from the dead may
serve to assure us that such is the appointment of
God: but it is by no means asserted that Christ
rose from the dead primarily and principally to
give us an assurance of a future state of retribution.

There are, therefore, in this proposition, two
assertions which remain to be proved: viz. That
the end or primary intention of Christ's death was
to bear testimony to the truth; and that the end
or primary intention of his resurrection from the
dead, was to afford us an assurance of a future
state of retribution. It is not, I hope, too much
to expect plain and positive proofs from Scripture
of these important points: especially as the Apostle
appears to speak a different language in his epistle
to the Romans, ch. iv. 25, where, speaking of
Jesus our Lord, whom God had raised from the
dead, he says; " Who was delivered for our of-
" fences, and raised again for our justification."

But you are sensible that the preceding summary does not comprehend all the tenets of Unitarianism, or even its distinguishing tenets; those

which relate to the *Person* and *Office* of the great author of our religion. This defect in your summary, as far as concerns the PERSON of Chrift, you proceed immediately to supply; telling us, that "Jesus was strictly and properly a human "Being, having no existence before his human "birth." *(Disc. p. 7.)* And presently after you say, that the term *Unitarian* properly belongs to those "who hold the simple humanity of Jesus." *(Disc. p. 8.)* In proof of this doctrine, you have not cited a single text of Scripture. Perhaps you might be led to think that this was unnecessary; the passages, in which his *humanity* is asserted, being so many and so obvious, that it cannot be disputed. Nor am I disposed to dispute it. We all, as well as you, believe that Jesus Christ was truly a man: this, therefore, is not the point in question: the thing to be proved, is, not the humanity, but the *simple* humanity of Jesus: the true question between us, is, Was Jesus Christ a mere man? or before his human birth did he exist in a nature superior to that of man? That the doctrine of the pre-existence and divinity of Christ is taught in the Scriptures, is, I think, evident, from the following passages: viz.

John i. 1. In the beginning was the Word, and the Word was with God, and the Word was God.—3. All things were made by him; and without him was not any thing made, that was made.—14. And the Word was made flesh, and dwelt among us.

John viii. 58. Jesus said unto them, Verily, verily, I say unto you, before Abraham was, I am.

John xvii. 5. And now, O Father, glorify thou me with thine own self, with the glory which I had with thee before the world was.

Philip. ii. 5, 6, 7, 8. Who, being in the form of God, thought it not robbery to be equal with God : but made himself of no reputation, and took upon him the form of a servant, and was made in the likeness of Men : and being found in fashion as a man, he humbled himself, and became obedient unto death, even the death of the cross.

Col. i. 15, 16, 17. Who is the image of the invisible God, the first-born of every creature : for by him were all things created, that are in heaven, and that are in earth, visible and invisible, whether they be thrones, or dominions, or principalities, or powers : all things are created by him, and for him ; and he is before all things, and by him all things consist.

Heb. i. 8. But unto the son he saith, Thy throne, O God, is for ever and ever.—10. And, Thou, Lord, in the beginning hast laid the foundation of the earth, and the heavens are the works of thine hands.

From the foregoing passages of scripture (to which many others might easily be added) it appears plain to my apprehension, that the Saviour of the world existed before his human birth in a nature infinitely superior to that of Man : and, in particular, that he was the Word of God, himself God, the I AM, who was before all things, and by whom all things were made.

Against this doctrine of the pre-existence of Christ you urge an argument, which not only in itself has no force, but is also taken up in direct opposition to the holy scriptures. You seem to be of opinion that the example of our Lord cannot be proposed to us with effect unless it be admitted that he was a mere man, liable to sin and suffering, and in all respects like unto his brethren. For you say, " I wish it were taken into " consideration by those who maintain it, (i. e. the " pre-existence) whether if we are not informed " by the Scriptures that the pre-existent spirit, " which is supposed to have dwelt in the human " body of Jesus, was liable to sin and suffering, " the opinion does not altogether oppose the ef- " ficacy of the example of Jesus." (Disc. p. 36.) You seem to impute to us the opinion that the divine Word, or whatever else you mean by the

term "pre-existent spirit," animated the body of
Jesus, supplying in him the place of a human
soul. But this is not the orthodox faith. We
believe that the divine Word assumed the whole
of the human nature; so that Christ is God and
Man in one person. " perfect God, and perfect
" Man, of a reasonable soul and human flesh
" subsisting." As God, I believe him to have
been impeccable : but when you argue that such
a belief " altogether opposes the efficacy of his
" example," surely you must have forgotten that
the example of God himself, of God the Father,
is in Scripture proposed to us for our imitation.
Eph. iv. 32. v. 1. " Be ye kind one to another,
" tender-hearted, forgiving one another even as
" God for Christ's sake hath forgiven you : Be ye
" therefore followers of God, as dear children."
And says our Lord himself, Matt. v. 44, 45.
" Love your enemies : bless them that curse you,
" do good to them that hate you, and pray for
" them which despitefully use you and persecute
" you : that ye may be the children of your Fa-
" ther which is heaven : for he maketh his sun to
" rise upon the evil and on the good, and sendeth
" rain on the just and on the unjust.—48. Be ye
" therefore perfect, even as your Father which is
" in heaven is perfect." With respect to the human nature of Christ, I am satisfied with the de-

claration of the Apostle, that he was "without "sin;" and I have no wish to enquire, whether this freedom from sin refers to the impeccability of his nature or to the innocency of his life. But I contend that neither the supposition of our Lord's impeccability, nor any other supposition, which tends to exalt the dignity of his nature, at all lessens the force of his example. His conduct is proposed to us either as the pattern according to which we are to fashion our own, or as our motive and encouragement to act as he did.— Considered as a pattern, the example cannot be too perfect, or proceed from too perfect a Being. Nor is its efficacy as a motive or encouragement at all diminished by the surpassing dignity of the Being to be imitated, in those instances more especially in which the example of Christ is proposed to us. The argument of the Apostle is, "Beloved, if God so loved us, we ought also to love one another." John iv. 11. And what stronger motive to brotherly love can be urged or conceived? How must we be excited to humility and acts of condescension, to even the meanest of our brethren, when we consider that the eternal Son of God himself, assuming our nature, did not disdain to minister to us his unworthy creatures? How must we be encouraged to bear without repining the hardships of po-

verty, and all the evils of a low condition, when
we look to the blessed Jesus, who, though he was
rich, yet for our sakes became poor ; and, when
he was upon earth, had not where to lay his
head. How can we give way to repining and
impatience, or grow weary and faint in our
minds under even the sharpest sufferings of this
present life, when we consider the spotless Lamb
of God, who endured such contradiction of sinners against himself, and patiently submitted to
the highest indignities, and to the severest tor-
ments which it is possible for man to suffer ?—
Who does not perceive, that in these and such
like instances, the efficacy of the example rises in
proportion to the dignity of the person in whose
steps we are exhorted to tread ?

The OFFICE of Christ you have no where,
as far as I recollect, distinctly stated. But I collect from certain expressions, which here and
there occur, that you believe him to have been
the Mediator, i. e. the medium of communication
between God and Men ; (*Disc. p. 7.*) but no
otherwise than as the Messenger of God to Men :
that the great object of his mission was to reveal
the doctrine of everlasting life, and to declare the
method by which everlasting life is to be obtained. (*Disc. p.* 30, *note.*) You do not distinctly state what this method is : but I suppose

it to be the practice of christian virtue; which you make to consist in the regulation of the affections and conduct by the precepts and example of Jesus. *(Disc. p. 19.)* You also state as a leading, though not the primary object of his mission, the offer of forgiveness upon repentance. *(Disc. p. 27.)*

That there is one Mediator between God and Men, the Man Christ Jesus;—that in the exercise of his mediatorial character he revealed to Men the will of God, and especially brought into light the doctrine of life and immortality;—that he delivered to us the precepts of a holy life, and hath shewn us by his own example how we may so walk as to please God;—and that he taught and commissioned his Apostles to teach in his name repentance and remission of sins to all nations, no Christian denies. On the contrary, we all thankfully acknowledge that to Jesus Christ, the great Prophet and Teacher of his people, it is alone owing that we are not like the Gentile world, ignorant of God and unacquainted with our duty; but are brought to the knowledge of the truth, and are instructed in the way of salvation. But has the Saviour no office but that of Prophet or Teacher? Is he called the Mediator between God and Men merely because he revealed the will of God to Men, and declared the way of salvation? The Apostle seems to have been of another mind, where (amidst his directions respecting prayers to be made for all men) having asserted that there is "one Mediator between "God and Men, the Man Christ Jesus," immediately adds, "who gave himself a ransom for "all:" which words plainly declare, not that he pointed out the way of salvation by his preaching; but that he effected a deliverance by his death: and, consequently, that he was the Mediator between God and Men, not only in the sense for which you contend, as a Prophet sent from God to announce his will to Men; but also as a Priest, appearing before God in behalf of Men, and making God propitious to them.

The priestly office of Christ, and the deliverance which he effected by his death, is utterly excluded from the unitarian creed. I cannot find in your whole book the death of Christ represented any otherwise than as an attestation of the truth of his doctrine: and you affirm that he is the propitiation for our sins, not because he propitiated God, but merely because he revealed the doctrine of pardon, and declared by what means the wrath of God might be averted, and his favour obtained: (*Disc. p.* 30.) and you endeavour to cast a slur upon the orthodox, by representing them as holding, that " because the

" Justice of God the Father *could* not be satisfied
" without a sacrifice of *infinite value*, therefore God
" the Son took upon him human nature, and by
" his sufferings as Man made atonement for the
" sins of Men." And again, that " the pardon of
" sins was purchased from the *inexorable* justice of
" the Father by the vicarious sufferings of the
" Son." *(Disc. p. 30.)* I am sorry to be obliged
to observe that this is a gross misrepresentation of
our doctrine. We believe that the eternal Son of
God assumed our nature, and in that nature became the sacrifice for our sins, and by an offering of his own blood averted from us the divine
wrath, and obtained for us God's favour and ac-
ceptance. And because Christ by dying for us
appeased the divine wrath, and removed every
obstacle in the way of our complete reconciliation
to God, therefore we say that he made satisfaction
for our sins. And more particularly because he
was set forth to be a propitiation, in order that
the divine Lawgiver might extend mercy to his
offending creatures without impeachment of his
justice ;* therefore we further say, that the death
of Christ satisfied the justice of God. But who
ever dreamed that the justice of God was inexorable ; or that this inexorable justice *could*
no otherwise be satisfied than by a sacrifice of

* See Rom. iii. 25, 26.

infinite value? If expressions to this purpose should unhappily have fallen from any advocate of the doctrine of satisfaction, let it, I pray you, be accounted an error of the individual, for which the orthodox in general are not answerable.— You yourself allow that the doctrine of satisfaction has appeared under two forms, the Calvinistic and the Arminian; the latter of which you pronounce to be less exceptionable and *unscriptural* than the former. (*Disc. p. 38.*) But I have not been able to discover that a sacrifice of infinite value, in order to satisfy the inexorable justice of God, is essential even to the Calvinistic form. Certainly Calvin, in his Institutes, lib. ii, cap. 6, where he expressly treats of this subject, asserts no such thing; but resolves the whole into the love of God. And with respect to our own Church, (for which I am more concerned,) we fetch not her opinions from the writings of individuals of her community, however eminent, but from her articles, her liturgy, and her homilies: and in them I find no such doctrine as that which you impute to us; viz. that the inexorable justice of God required for its satisfaction a sacrifice of infinite value. And, after all, the doctrine of satisfaction is itself only a form of the doctrine of atonement by the blood of Christ. For it refers not to the thing itself

effected by Christ's blood, which we affirm to be
our reconciliation with God; but merely to the
manner in which we suppose this effect to have
been produced. And since an error as to this
point does not affect the main question, (for the
thing itself might still be true, notwithstanding
we had misconceived the manner in which it was
effected) it follows that your argument, in order
to be successful, must be directed against the
doctrine itself; and not merely against the form
under which it is commonly represented.

But the doctrine itself, under whatever form
it appears, you consider as an error which gives
support to numerous other errors of religious
belief: and you think it not too much to assert that
when once this is given up, and scriptural (i. e.
unitarian) views of the subject adopted, christian
morality will have its due weight, and faith be
easily brought nearly, if not altogether, to the
level of gospel truth:" (Disc. p. 38.) i. e. Men
would become almost, if not altogether, Unitarians. But whence, sir, this decided hostility
against a doctrine, which has been joyfully em-
braced by the wisest and the best in all ages of the
Christian Church; and has been found to afford
the greatest encouragement and support to the re-
turning sinner, in all his applications for mercy to
the throne of grace? You state your reasons ge-

nerally. You tell us, that it is a doctrine "fraught
" in all its forms with baneful consequences re-
" specting our ideas both of the character of the
" only God, and of the nature and design of that
" revelation of his will which he made to man by
" Jesus Christ." And you affirm, that " if pur-
" sued to its just conclusions, as it ought to be,
" or be given up, there would be an end to all
" scriptural foundation for the love of God and
" for Christian practice." (*Dise p.* 38.) You tell
us not what those baneful consequences are, with
which this doctrine is so heavily laden; nor what
those conclusions are, to which it might and
ought to be pursued; and I am not at liberty to
look for them in the writings of other Unitarians.
But I strongly suspect that they refer to the form,
under which you have chosen to represent our
doctrine; viz. that the inexorable justice of God
required a satisfaction of infinite value, rather than
to the doctrine as we really hold it: and consequently they affect not the question.

But were it otherwise, I beg to remind you
that agreeably to your own principles, a doctrine
is not to be rejected merely because it may not accord with our own reasonings upon the subject:
the great question is, have we sufficient reason to
believe that it was taught either immediately or
mediately by Jesus? " Give us," you say, "but

"sufficient evidence of this, and we will humbly
"exert ourselves to cast down reasonings, and every
"high thing that exalts itself against the knowledge
"of God, and to bring into captivity every thought
"to the obedience of Christ." *(Disc. p. 11.)* Feeling as I do the importance of the doctrine of atonement, and thinking with you that it is the very bulwark of orthodoxy, I will endeavour to give you the satisfaction which you require, and proceed to state the scriptural evidence upon which I myself receive this doctrine, and which appears to me abundantly sufficient to prove that it is worthy of all men to be received.

In speaking of spiritual and heavenly things, of which, in our present state, we cannot have distinct and adequate ideas, we are under the necessity of employing, and the Holy Ghost, in condescension to our capacity, employs in Scripture, terms and names which properly belong to earthly and sensible objects, such as fall within the compass of our knowledge and experience. Thus we all speak of the wrath or anger of God: but we do not mean to ascribe to the Deity, the passion which we call Anger; for we know that the Deity is without passions: But because there is in the Deity an attribute which answers to this passion—something which causes him to reject from his favour whatever is offensive to his pure and holy na-

ture—something which is to the Deity what anger
is to man, we on account of this analogy call it
by the same name. In like manner, when the object of the divine displeasure is no longer rejected,
but becomes an object of favour, we scruple not
to say, in the same analogical sense, that the divine anger is pacified; that God is propitiated and
reconciled.

From the Epistle to the Hebrews, we learn,
that the Mosaical dispensation was merely tempo-
rary; and was ordained solely for the purpose of
typifying and prefiguring a better state of things to
follow, of which it is expressly called the example, the pattern, the shadow: and it appears, not
from a few detached passages, but from the whole
tenor of the epistle, that the Apostle's intention
was to shew the excellency of the latter above the
former, by a comparison of the two in their corresponding parts; and the relations which they
bear to each other in various instances, is not
merely implied, but expressly declared. The
same Office in the heavenly dispensation is ascribed
to Christ, as was discharged by the High-Priest
under the law: and his blood is made to corres-
pond in virtue and efficacy with that of the legal
victims. Here then are analogies, which, when
pursued to their just conclusions, can hardly fail
to determine the great point in dispute. This sub-

ject is continued through the greater part of the
epistle: I shall at present select a few passages in
which the analogy is expressly asserted.

Heb. v. 1—5. Every High-Priest, taken from
among men, is ordained for men in things pertaining to God, that he may offer both gifts and
sacrifices for sins: Who can have compassion on
the ignorant, and on them that are out of the way;
for that he himself also is compassed with infir-
mity. And by reason hereof, he ought, as for the
people, so also for himself, to offer for sins. And
no man taketh this honour to himself, but he that
is called of God, as was Aaron. So also Christ
glorified not himself to be made an High-Priest;
but he that said unto him, Thou art my Son, to-
day have I begotten thee.

Ch. vii. 26, 27. Such an High-Priest became
us, who is holy, harmless, undefiled, separate from
sinners, and made higher than the heavens; who
needeth not daily, as those High-Priests, to offer
up sacrifice, first for his own sins, and then for the
people's: for this he did once, when he offered up
himself.

Ch. viii. 1—3. We have such an High-Priest
who is set on the right hand of the throne of the
Majesty in the heavens; a minister of the sanctu-
ary, and of the true tabernacle, which the Lord
pitched, and not man. For every High-Priest is

ordained to offer gifts and sacrifices; wherefore it is of necessity that this man have somewhat also to offer.

Ch. ix. 6—12. Now when these things were thus ordained, the Priests went always into the first tabernacle, accomplishing the service of God; but into the second went the High-Priest alone once every year, not without blood, which he offered for himself, and for the errors of the people: the Holy Ghost this signifying, that the way into the holiest of all was not yet made manifest, while as the first tabernacle was yet standing: which was a figure for the time then present, in which were offered both gifts and sacrifices, that could not make him that did the service perfect, as pertaining to the conscience; which stood only in meats and drinks, and divers washings, and carnal ordinances, imposed on them until the time of reformation. But Christ being come an High-Priest of good things to come, by a greater and more perfect tabernacle, not made with hands, that is to say, not of this building; neither by the blood of goats and calves, but by his own blood, he entered in once into the holy place, having obtained eternal redemption for us.

Ch. x. 11—14. And every Priest standeth daily ministering and offering oftentimes the same sacrifices, which can never take away sins:

But this man, after he had offered one sacrifice for sins, for ever sat down on the right hand of God; from henceforth expecting till his enemies be made his footstool. For by one offering he hath perfected for ever them that are sanctified.

In the foregoing passages there is most clearly ascribed to Christ, an office, corresponding with that which the High-Priest discharged in the earthly tabernacle. Like the legal High-Priests, he was called of God, and ordained for men: like them he made an offering for sin; but, with this difference, that they offered the blood of brute beasts, whereas he offered his own blood: and more especially, it is declared, that the office of Christ is analogous to that of the High-Priest on the great day of expiation; but, with this difference, that in order to make the service in the legal tabernacle effectual, there was required a repetition of it once every year; whereas the corresponding effect, in the Christian dispensation, was produced by a single offering.

The ceremonies, observed on the day of expiation, are described at large in the sixteenth chapter of Leviticus; from which it appears that the High-Priest was accustomed on that day to go within the vail into the inner tabernacle, with the blood of the appointed victims: by the offering of which, he consecrated anew the whole Jewish economy, cleansed the people from the uncleanness and the sins which would otherwise have cut them off from communion with God, and made them a holy people, capable of appearing before God, and of paying to him an acceptable service. So that the High-Priest was manifestly a mediator or intercessor between God and the people: to both of whom the service, which he performed in the inner tabernacle, had respect: It respected the people, whom it sanctified and cleansed from legal uncleanness, and put in a condition of holding communion with God: and it respected God, whom it propitiated, and caused to look upon the people, thus cleansed, with an eye of favour. And not only the sacrifices offered on the day of expiation, but also all the sin-offerings under the law, had this double respect: for all the atonements were made *to* God *for* the people; to God, that he might be reconciled and become propitious; for the people, that they might be cleansed and made fit for his service. A corresponding, but much more efficacious power, is ascribed to the blood of Christ, in the following remarkable passage:

Heb. ix. 13, 14. For if the blood of bulls and of goats, and the ashes of an heifer, sprinkling the unclean, sanctifieth to the purifying of the flesh; how much more shall the blood of Christ, who through the eternal spirit offered himself without spot to God, purge your conscience from dead works to serve the living God.

After the analogy expressly asserted in the foregoing passage, there can be no doubt of the sense in which the following ought to be taken.

Eph. v. 25—27. Christ also loved the Church and gave himself for it, that he might sanctify and cleanse it with the washing of water by the word; that he might present it to himself a glorious Church, not having spot, or wrinkle, or any such thing, but that it should be holy and without blemish.

Tit. ii. 14. Who gave himself for us that he might redeem us from all iniquity, and purify unto himself a peculiar people zealous of good works.

Heb. x. 10. By the which will we are sanctified through the offering of the body of Jesus Christ once for all.

1 John, i. 7. If we walk in the light, as he is in the light, we have fellowship one with another; and the blood of Jesus Christ his son cleanseth us from all sin.

Rev. i. 5. Unto him that loved us, and washed us from our sins in his own blood.

Matt. xxvi. 28. This is my blood of the New Testament, which is shed for many for the remission of sins.

Rom. iii. 23—25. For all have sinned and come short of the glory of God; being justified freely by his grace through the redemption that is in Jesus Christ; whom God hath set forth to be a propitiation through faith in his blood.

Heb. ii. 17. Wherefore in all things it behoved him to be made like unto his brethren, that he might be a merciful and faithful High Priest in things pertaining to God, to make reconciliation for the sins of the people.

Rom. v. 10. If, when we were enemies, we were reconciled to God by the death of his Son; much more, being reconciled, we shall be saved by his life.

Eph. ii. 13—16. But now in Christ Jesus, ye, who sometimes were far off, are made nigh by the blood of Christ. For he is our peace, who hath made both one, and hath broken down the middle wall of partition between us; having abolished in his flesh the enmity, even the law of commandments contained in ordinances; for to make in himself of twain one new man, so making peace; and that he might reconcile both unto God in one body by the cross, having slain the enmity thereby.

Col. i. 20. Having made peace through the blood of his cross, by him to reconcile all things to himself.

1 John, ii. 1, 2, If any man sin, we have an advocate with the Father, Jesus Christ the righteous: and he is the propitiation for our sins; and not for ours only, but also for the sins of the whole world.

1 John, iv. 10. Herein is love, not that we loved God, but that he loved us, and sent his Son to be the propitiation for our sins.

From these passages it appears, that the blood of Christ has the power, both of sanctifying and cleansing the offender, and also of propitiating God; i. e. in other words, it has the power of making atonement to God for sinners.

There are also in scripture other analogies, in which the part, assigned to the death of Christ, proves most powerfully, that it has an immediate effect in procuring our reconciliation with God. The principal are those in which the death of Christ is denominated a ransom and a price.

Matt. xx. 28. The Son of Man came not to be ministered unto, but to minister, and to give his life a ransom for many.

Eph. i. 7. In whom we have redemption through his blood, the forgiveness of sins.

1 Tim. ii. 6. Who gave himself a ransom for all.

1 Pet. i. 18, 19. Ye were not redeemed with corruptible things, as silver and gold, from your

vain conversation, received by tradition from your fathers; but with the precious blood of Christ, as of a lamb without blemish and without spot.

2 Pet. ii. 1. There shall be false teachers among you, who privily shall bring in damnable heresies, even denying the Lord that bought them. 1 Cor. vi. 20.

Rev. v. 9. Thou wast slain and hast redeemed to God by thy blood.

Hence it appears, that as the ransom is to the redemption of a captive, and the price to the purchase of a possession, so is the blood of Christ to the deliverance of sinners from the power of sin and death: and since the redemption is immediately owing to the ransom, and the purchase to the price, we can be at no loss to determine what effect is to be ascribed to the death of Christ in the deliverance of sinners.

Another representation of the death of Christ is that of a punishment inflicted on account of our sins.

Isaiah liii. 6. The Lord hath laid on him the iniquity of us all.

Rom. v. 6. When we were yet without strength, in due time Christ died for the ungodly. v. 8.

2 Cor. v. 21. For he hath made him to be sin for us, who knew no sin; that we might be made the righteousness of God in him.

Gal. iii. 13. Christ hath redeemed us from the curse of the law, being made a curse for us.

Heb. ix. 28. Christ was once offered to bear the sins of many.

1 Pet. ii. 24. Who his own self bare our sins in his own body on the tree, that we, being dead to sins, should live unto righteousness: by whose stripes ye were healed.

1 Pet. iii. 18. For Christ also hath once suffered for sins, the just for the unjust, that he might bring us to God.

From all which passages of Scripture, taken together, it plainly appears, that our Saviour Christ, though himself without sin, condescended to suffer as a malefactor, in order to deliver us from that curse and punishment which the law had denounced against sin: and, therefore, to *his* sufferings *our* deliverance is immediately owing.

There is another subject upon which I beg to say a few words. You affirm that God (meaning the supreme God, the Father of our Lord Jesus Christ,) is the only proper object of religious worship *(Disc. p. 7.)*—that many of our Lord's followers have wrongly appreciated the rank which he held in the scale of Being; and have consequently rendered him honours which he never claimed; and have thus encroached upon the unrivalled supremacy of the only God. *(Disc. p. 19.)*

We have already considered our Lord's rank in the scale of Being before his incarnation; and from the passages of Scripture then produced, it is, I think, apparent, that he was the Word or Son of God, himself God, antecedent to all things, and the Maker of all things. I shall now call your attention to a few passages, which refer to his condition since his resurrection.

Matt. xxviii. 18. All power is given unto me in heaven and in earth.

Mark xvi. 19. So then after the Lord had spoken unto them, he was received up into heaven, and sat on the right hand of God.

John v. 22. The Father judgeth no man, but hath committed all judgment unto the Son.

2 Cor. v. 10. We must all appear before the judgment seat of Christ.

Phil. ii. 9—11. Wherefore God also hath highly exalted him, and given him a name which is above every name; that at the name of Jesus every knee should bow, of things in heaven, and things in earth, and things under the earth; and that every tongue should confess that Jesus Christ is Lord, to the glory of God the Father. Eph. i. 20.

Tit. ii. 13. Looking for that blessed hope, and the glorious appearing of the great God and our Saviour Jesus Christ.*

* See Granville Sharp's Remarks on the uses of the Definitive Article; and Wordsworth's Six Letters to Granville Sharp, Esq.

Heb. i. 3. Who being the brightness of his glory, and the express image of his person, and upholding all things by the word of his power, when he had by himself purged our sins, sat down on the right hand of the Majesty on high.

Heb. ii. 9. We see Jesus, who was made a little lower than the angels for the suffering of death, crowned with glory and honour.

Rev. v. 12. Worthy is the lamb that was slain to receive power, and riches, and wisdom, and strength, and honour, and glory, and blessing.

Such being the dignity and power to which the God-Man Christ Jesus is now exalted, there can, I think, be little hesitation respecting the meaning of those passages which relate to the honours which he claimed, or which have been supposed to be due to him.

John v. 23. That all men should honour the Son, even as they honour the Father.

Acts. vii. 59. And they stoned Stephen, calling upon God, and saying, Lord Jesus, receive my spirit.

Acts ix. 14. And here he hath authority from the chief Priests to bind all that call on thy name.

Rom. x. 13. Whosoever shall call upon the name of the Lord shall be saved.

1 Cor. i. 2, 3. To them that are sanctified in Christ Jesus, called to be saints, with all that in

every place call upon the name of Jesus Christ our Lord, both their's and our's; grace be unto you, and peace from God our Father and from the Lord Jesus Christ.

Gal. vi. 18. The grace of our Lord Jesus Christ be with your spirit.

2 Thes. ii. 16, 17. Now our Lord Jesus Christ himself, and God, even our Father, which hath loved us and hath given us everlasting consolation and good hope through grace, comfort your hearts and stablish you in every good word and work.

2 Pet. iii 18. To him be glory both now and for ever. Amen.

Rev. i. 6. To him be glory and dominion for ever and ever. Amen.

Rev. v. 13. Blessing, and honour, and glory, and power, be unto him that sitteth upon the throne, and unto the Lamb, for ever and ever.

And thus it appears, that our Lord claimed to himself the same honour which men were accustomed to pay to the Father; and, from the examples recorded in scripture, we are taught, that to him prayer is to be addressed, and glory to be ascribed: in which two acts, divine worship principally consists.

In the preceding pages I have endeavoured to shew, in opposition to Unitarianism, 1st. That Jesus Christ, the great author of our religion, was not a mere man, having no existence before his human birth; but that he pre-existed in a nature infinitely more excellent; being the Word or Son of God, himself God, who was before all things, and by whom all things were made; who for us men and for our salvation condescended to divest himself of the glory of the Godhead, and to take our nature upon him, and to be born into the world. 2dly. That he appeared in the world not only as a Prophet sent to reveal the will of God, and to announce the blessings and privileges of the Christian covenant; but also as our Priest, from whose gracious interposition in our behalf we derive our title to the blessings and privileges, which, as our Prophet, he announced:—and further, that he submitted to death, not only to attest the truth and to confirm the doctrine which he taught, but principally to make an atonement for us, to cleanse us from the defilements of sin, and to make us acceptable to God. 3dly. That religious worship is not confined to God the Father, but is due also to God the Son, who, as well as the Prophet and Priest, is also the Lord and King of his Church and People, to whom all power is given, and who exercises absolute sovereignty over the whole creation for the benefit of his Church.

I beg to add a few words respecting the names and titles, which are attributed in the scriptures to the blessed Jesus. Unitarians have been charged with rejecting some of these names, because they do not accord with their own sentiments. *(Disc. p. 20.)* You do not absolutely deny this charge; for you declare that there are some names which you seldom employ, unless when you have an opportunity of stating in what way you use them. And indeed, the very scantiness of your Creed obliges you to great caution in this respect; otherwise you might be supposed to hold opinions, which in fact you reject. Even the title, which very commonly occurs in scripture, and is most in common use,—that of Saviour—you cannot employ in its primary meaning, but only in a lower and secondary sense; for according to your doctrine Jesus is called the Saviour, not because he saved his people from their sins,* but because he communicated the way of salvation. *(Disc. p. 31.)*

But to my apprehension the very caution, which you are obliged to use in a case of this importance, militates most powerfully against your opinions. The gospel was not intended for the Few, for philosophers and men of learning, who can refine and explain away, till words, which have apparently much meaning, come to signify nothing: but it was intended for mankind in general, of whom the Many are poor and illiterate, having their un-

* See Matt. i. 21.

derstanding open to the plain and obvious sense of words, but incapable of nice distinctions and subtile refinements: and to suppose that such distinctions and refinements are necessary to explain the way of salvation, is in effect to assert that the scriptures were given, not to instruct, but to lead into error. On the other hand, it is no little recommendation of the orthodox doctrine that it is derived from the obvious sense of scripture. What is there revealed concerning Christ and his salvation, that we humbly receive and firmly hold: And we give him the honour due unto his name. We acknowledge him to be the Son of God and the Son of Man—the Lord of Glory and the Servant of God—we believe in him as our Saviour and Redeemer, our Mediator and Intercessor, our Lord and our King: and these titles we ascribe to him in their true and primary sense, without limitation or reserve.

You labour to prove that Unitarianism is peculiarly adapted to call forth our best affections, and to inspire us with the truest love to Christ and veneration for his character. (*Disc. p.* 22.) But to me there appears in the Unitarian scheme comparatively little which interests, little which animates. If I could consider Christ merely as the Messenger of God, the commission with which he was charged, and the powers of which he was possessed, would indeed entitle him to my reverence and attention, while his boldness and patient suffering in the cause of truth would excite my admiration and esteem. But I should hardly feel that wonder, love, and joy which my present faith cannot fail of exciting in every true believer.—— That the everlasting Son of the everlasting Father, who had dwelt from all eternity in light unapproachable, should lay aside the glory of the Godhead, and become a minister to man upon earth—— that he should assume our mortal nature, and after a life of poverty and sorrow should die an ignominious death; and all for us miserable sinners, that he might deliver us from death, and exalt us to everlasting life:——Who, at the contemplation of these things, is not lost in wonder at such astonishing love and condescension? Who is not ready to exclaim with David, Lord, what is man that thou art thus mindful of him? Who does not feel in his own bosom a sacred fire, bursting forth into acts of praise and adoration? Thou, O blessed Jesu, art indeed a Saviour! Thou excellest in love! Thou aboundest in grace! Thy name is deservedly above every name: Worthy is the Lamb that was slain to receive power, and honour, and glory, and blessing; and therefore blessing, and honour, and glory, and power, be unto him that sitteth upon the throne, and unto the Lamb for ever and ever.

Nor do the affections thus called forth by the contemplation of the Saviour's love, at all derogate, as you seem to imagine, from those with which we ought to regard " the Father who sent him." *(Disc. p. 29.)* We acknowledge with heartfelt joy and thankfulness, that it was the undeserved love of God which alone moved him to send his Son into the world: We impute it solely to his pity and forbearance, that the punishment, denounced against sin, was not immediately executed; that in the midst of judgment God remembered mercy, for the exercise of which he was graciously pleased to open a way, by appointing a propitiation for sin: and we humbly submit to the method of reconciliation which he hath appointed; looking up to him as our reconciled God and Father, in the fullest confidence, that he, who spared not his own Son, but delivered him up for us all, will also with him freely give us all things: that he will give us grace to repent, and to turn from our sins; that he will freely pardon the sins of which we have so repented; that he will cleanse and sanctify our polluted nature; will assist us in the performance of our duty; will accept our sincere, though imperfect, services; and will finally receive us into the mansions of everlasting blessedness; not, indeed, for any thing in us deserving such a reward; but through him who died for our

sins, and was raised again for our justification,
and is now at the right hand of God, where he
ever liveth, making intercession for us.

" Without controversy, great is the mystery of
" godliness !"* Nor could it well be otherwise.
For the thoughts of God are not as our thoughts,
neither are his ways our ways. In vain then does
man attempt to bring down the divine proceedings
to the level of his own limited understanding. It
more becomes him not to be wise above that which
is written, but to bow with all humility to the
authority of God's word. You, sir, profess to acknowledge this authority, and declare your readi-
ness to admit what shall appear to be true, however opposite to your own preformed opinions.
(*Disc. p.* 8.) You will, I trust, retain this spirit,
when you take a review of the great and important
doctrines, to which I have now been endeavouring
to call your attention. And may the great Teacher
of wisdom lead you into all the truth, and make
you to " grow in grace, and in the knowledge of
" our Lord and Saviour Jesus Christ. To him be
" glory both now and for ever. Amen."†

* 1 Tim. iii. 16.   † 2 Pet. iii. 18.

TREWMANS, PRINTERS, EXETER.

ERRATA.

Page 11, line 25, read *was* raised.

13,   10, dele 5.

23, for *are* read *were*.

15,   23, read *in* heaven.

16,   20, read 1 John iv. 11.

24,   16, for *distant* read *distinct*.

www.ingramcontent.com/pod-product-compliance
Lightning Source LLC
Chambersburg PA
CBHW081304040426
42452CB00014B/2642